THEMATIC UNIT
FRIENDSHIP

Written by Janet Hale

Illustrated by Sue Fullam

Teacher Created Materials, Inc.

P.O. Box 1040

Huntington Beach, CA 92647

©1991 Teacher Created Materials, Inc.

Made in U.S.A.

ISBN 1-55734-274-1

Table of Contents

3061200030388

Introduction

Friendship contains a captivating whole language, thematic unit about being and having friends. Its 80 exciting, reproducible pages are filled with a wide variety of lesson ideas designed for use with primary children. At its core are two high-quality children's literature selections, *Friends* and *Best Friends*. For each of these books activities are included which set the stage for reading, encourage the enjoyment of the book, and extend the concepts gained. In addition, the theme is connected to the curriculum with activities in language arts (including daily writing suggestions), math, science, social studies, art, music, and life skills (cooking, physical education, etc.). Many of these activities encourage cooperative learning. Suggestions and patterns for bulletin boards and unit management tools are additional time savers for the busy teacher. Furthermore, directions for student-created Big Books and a culminating activity, which allow students to synthesize their knowledge in order to produce products that can be shared beyond the classroom, highlight this very complete teacher resource.

This thematic unit includes:

- **literature selections** — summaries of two children's books with related lessons (complete with reproducible pages) that cross the curriculum

- **poetry** — suggested selections and lessons enabling students to write and publish their own works

- **planning guides** — suggestions for sequencing lessons each day of the unit

- **language experience ideas** — daily suggestions as well as activities across the curriculum, including Big Books

- **bulletin board ideas** — suggestions and plans for student-created and/or interactive bulletin boards

- **homework suggestions** — extending the unit to the child's home

- **curriculum connections** — in language arts, math, science, social studies, art, music, and life skills such as cooking

- **group projects** — to foster cooperative learning

- **a culminating activity** — which requires students to synthesize their learning to produce a product or engage in an activity that can be shared with others

- **a bibliography** — suggesting additional literature and nonfiction books on the theme

> **To keep this valuable resource intact so that it can be used year after year, you may wish to punch holes in the pages and store them in a three-ring binder.**

Introduction *(cont.)*

Why Whole Language?

A whole language approach involves children in using all modes of communication: reading, writing, listening, observing, illustrating, experiencing, and doing. Communication skills are interconnected and integrated into lessons that emphasize the whole of language rather than isolating its parts. The lessons revolve around selected literature. Reading is not taught as a separate subject from writing and spelling, for example. A child reads, writes (spelling appropriately for his/her level), speaks, listens, etc. in response to a literature experience introduced by the teacher. In this way, language skills grow naturally, stimulated by involvement and interest in the topic at hand.

Why Thematic Planning?

One very useful tool for implementing an integrated whole language program is thematic planning. By choosing a theme with correlating literature selections for a unit of study, a teacher can plan activities throughout the day that lead to a cohesive, in-depth study of the topic. Students will be practicing and applying their skills in meaningful contexts. Consequently, they will tend to learn and retain more. Both teachers and students will be freed from a day that is broken into unrelated segments of isolated drill and practice.

Why Cooperative Learning?

Besides academic skills and content, students need to learn social skills. No longer can this area of development be taken for granted. Students must learn to work cooperatively in groups in order to function well in modern society. Group activities should be a regular part of school life and teachers should consciously include social objectives as well as academic objectives in their planning. For example, a group working together to write a report may need to select a leader. The teacher should make clear to the students and monitor the qualities of good leader-follower group interaction just as he/she would state and monitor the academic goals of the project.

Why Big Books?

An excellent cooperative, whole language activity is the production of Big Books. Groups of students, or the whole class, can apply their language skills, content knowledge, and creativity to produce a Big Book that can become a part of the classroom library to be read and reread. These books make excellent culminating projects for sharing beyond the classroom with parents, librarians, other classes, etc. Big Books can be produced in many ways and this thematic unit book includes directions for at least one method you may choose.

Friends

by Helme Heine

Summary

Friends are so much fun to be with! In this delightful story of friendship you will meet Charlie Rooster, Johnny Mouse, and Percy, the pig. They wake up the barnyard, go for a morning bike ride, play hide-and-go seek, pretend to be pirates, go fishing, pig out (no pun intended!) on cherries, and pledge to be friends forever!

The outline below is a suggested plan for using the various activities presented in this unit. You may adapt the ideas to meet specific needs in your classroom environment.

Sample Plan

Day I

- Brainstorm "What Is a Friend?" (p. 6)
- Bulletin Board Display (p. 63)
- Read *Friends*
- Friendly Observations (p. 6)
- Build a Friend (pp. 9-11)
- Write "My Friends" Book (p. 29)
- "Friends Across the Wall" Art Project (p. 51)
- Homework—Picture This! (p. 56)

Day II

- Share Homework
- Create a "Fun Times" Web (p. 6)
- "Friends Are Fun!" Activity (p. 12)
- Friendship Exercise Course (p. 53)
- Create Math Games (p. 41)
- Make Friendship Fudge (p. 54)
- Friends Are Fun Acrostic (p. 28)
- Homework—Let's Have Fun! (p. 56)

Day III

- Share Homework
- Friendship Wheels (p. 13)
- "Befriend" Another Class (p. 7)
- Practice Math Facts (p. 41)
- "Be a Friend" Posters (p. 30)

- Listen to a Community Friend (p. 7)
- Write Friendly Thank You Letters (p. 7)
- Homework—Helper Coupons (p. 56)

Day IV

- What Is a Friend? Review Activity (p. 15)
- If We Were All the Same - Pre-Reading Activity (p. 16)
- A Friendly "Round" of Song (p. 28)
- How Are We Different? (p. 47)
- "I Can Be Different" Accordion Books (p. 29)
- Friends Across the Globe (p. 50)
- Homework—Same/Different Chart (p. 56)

Day V

- Culminating Activity: Create a Friendship Listening Center (p. 57)
- Hand out a Friendship Award (page 77) to each student.

Overview of Activities

SETTING THE STAGE

1. What is a friend? Brainstorm with students what they believe the qualities of a friend are. Encourage students to recognize that classmates, family members, people in their neighborhood, and even animals can be their friends! Write their ideas on butcher paper.

Don't Be Square–Be A Friend!

2. To prepare your classroom for the friendship unit, assemble the bulletin board display outlined on pages 63-68. Complete the suggested introduction activity.

3. Create a web with the students entitled "Fun Times." Ask the students to give as many examples as they can of ways in which they have fun being with their friends. Note: Remember that a friend does not necessarily mean a classmate—a friend can have four legs and wag its tail, too!

4. Make a graph of your students' friends. Give each student two square-shaped sticky note pad sheets. Have them draw the face of two of their friends. Make a graph form labeled male, female, and animal. Have students come up and place their sticky note sheets above the appropriate titles. When all students have placed their sheets, study the results. Encourage mathematical comparisons; for example, "More students in our class have friends that are girls, than friends that are boys."

ENJOYING THE BOOK

1. When reading the story, *Friends*, explain that you want your students to notice how each of the three characters showed he was a friend, both by the text and picture clues. After the initial reading, list observations on paper "headed" by the animals' faces (patterns on page 8). Post their findings in the classroom with the title "Friendly Observations."

2. Have children act out the story as a play or use the faces on page 8 as stick puppets to retell it. To make stick puppets: Copy the faces onto tagboard and have students color appropriately. Cut out and staple to a tongue depressor or craft stick.

3. Discuss or review the concept of quotation marks. Quotation marks tell us when someone, or a group of characters, is talking in a story. Review the story and write out the sentences that the three friends say. They will be: "Good friends always stick together," "Good friends always decide things together," "Friends are always fair," "Sometimes good friends can't be together." Have a group discussion about what the three friends meant by each comment. Provide paper and have students write their own friendship sentences. Share sentences with the class. Post sentences around a student-drawn illustration of the *Friends* book cover!

6

Overview of Activities *(cont.)*

4. Cooperation is very important in friendship and in working together in the classroom. Discuss how the three animals cooperated to make the bicycle work. Divide the class into cooperative teams of three or four. Have them draw a picture and write about a machine or vehicle that they could operate by working together. Have each team share their picture and sentences. Display the cooperative works of art and sentences in the hallway.

EXTENDING THE BOOK

1. Friends help each other. Percy, Johnny Mouse, and Charlie Rooster enjoyed helping each other. Arrange for your class to go to another classroom (preferably a lower grade) to help the students in that class learn or review a new skill, or have a shared-reading experience.

2. Friends care about each other. Important friends in our neighborhood are our community workers. The police officers, fire fighters, doctors, dentists, and other service providers are our friends. They help us by keeping us safe and well. Invite a special guest to come to the class and discuss his/her job and how he/she is our friend.

3. After having a community friend come and talk to the class, have the students write thank you letters to show their friendliness to others! Provide writing paper and large construction paper to create Thank You cards (see illustration below).

A student-drawn picture

folded 11" x 18" colored construction paper decorated by student

writing paper →

Dear Policeman Bob,

Thank you for coming to our class and for being a friend.

Love Sara C.

Friends' Faces

*See suggested activities page 6.

Faces can be used as stick puppets.

8

Build a Friend

Create an imaginary friend! Pick your new friend below. Color and cut out. Using the following pages, cut out the clothes and activities that you want your friend to have. Share your new friend with someone in the room. See who has a friend like yours. Maybe you can be new friends, too!

Build a Friend *(cont.)*

10

Build a Friend *(cont.)*

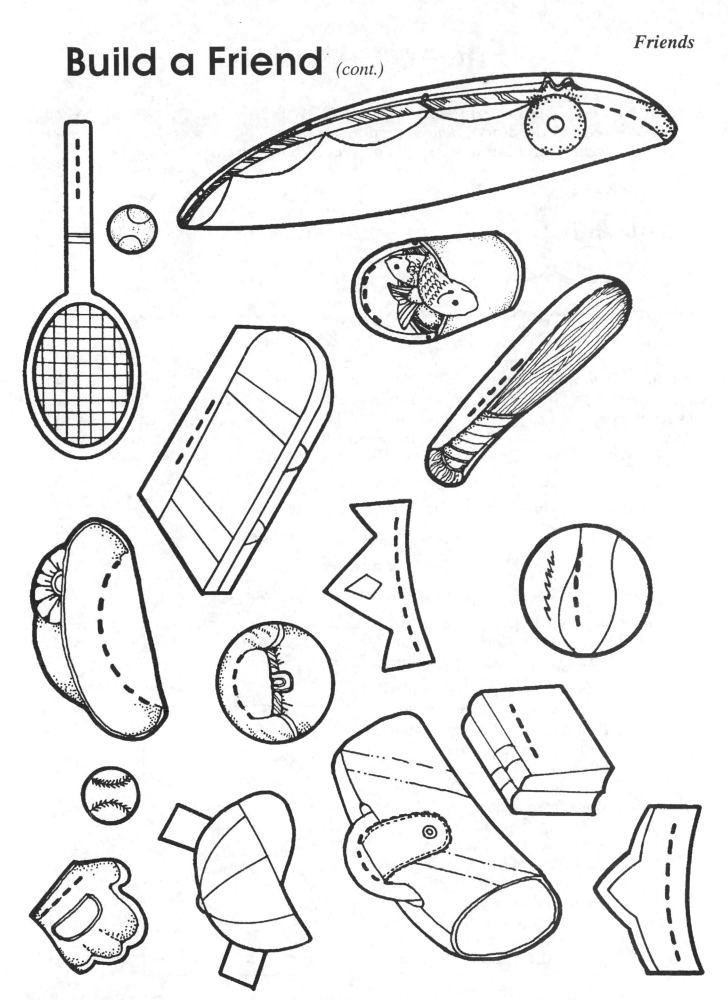

11

Friends Are Fun!

Preparation: Complete the "Fun Times" web (p. 6). With the "Fun Times" web posted, re-read the story *Friends*. Add to the web all of the ways in which the three friends had fun together (if not already on the web).

wake up the farm animals	ride a bicycle	play hide and go seek
play pirates	ride in a boat	catch fish
look for cherries	eat	sit and rest
talk	try to spend the night	dream about each other

Let students know that they can have more fun if they follow these rules:

Take turns being the leader.

Cooperate with each other.

Be a good friend—help others.

Check to see if Percy, Johnny Mouse, and Charlie Rooster followed these three "Be a Friend Rules" by reviewing the story. Ask students to give examples of when they have followed these rules in the classroom, school, home, or neighborhood.

Activity: Copy the three rules onto cloud shapes (pattern p. 69). Post them in the classroom. Place a basket of blank Friendship Stars nearby. (Use the pattern on p. 70 to cut stars from yellow construction paper). Whenever the teacher or students catch a friend following a Friendship Rule, the friend may take a star from the basket and write his/her name on it and place it near the appropriate cloud.

12

Helping Friends

Friends Help Each Other

Ask the students to think of times when they have helped friends. Give an example of a time that you helped a friend. Ask students to give examples of how the animals in the story helped each other. List their replies on butcher paper.

* Johnny Mouse and Percy helped Charlie Rooster wake up the barnyard animals.
* To ride the bike, Charlie Rooster steered while Percy and Johnny Mouse pedaled.
* Johnny Mouse steered the boat, while Charlie Rooster helped it sail, and Percy covered up the hole in the bottom of the boat with his body.
* Percy held Johnny Mouse while the mouse used his tail to go fishing, and Charlie Rooster took care of the worms in his beak.
* They all helped each other to reach the cherries by standing on each other's shoulders.
* Johnny Mouse and Percy helped Charlie Rooster's anger by giving him the cherry pits.
* Percy helped Charlie Rooster get unstuck from Johnny Mouse's "house" hole.
* They helped each other decide that it was not the best idea to spend the night together; instead, they could dream about each other, as true friends do!

When Friends Help Each Other, They Are Cooperating.

Explain the above statement to the class. Ask students to give examples of how they help each other (cooperate) in the classroom. Add their replies to the butcher paper.

Hand out a **Friendship Wheel** (p. 14) to each student.

Give the following directions:

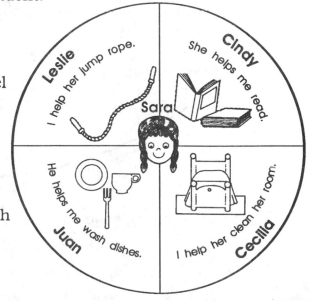

1. In the center, where the smaller circle is located, draw a picture of yourself and label with your name.

2. Think of four friends that you help, or that help you. Write their names in the four sections.

3. Draw a picture and/or write a sentence expressing how you or your friend help each other.

4. Share wheels either in whole or small groups. Display.

Friendship Wheel

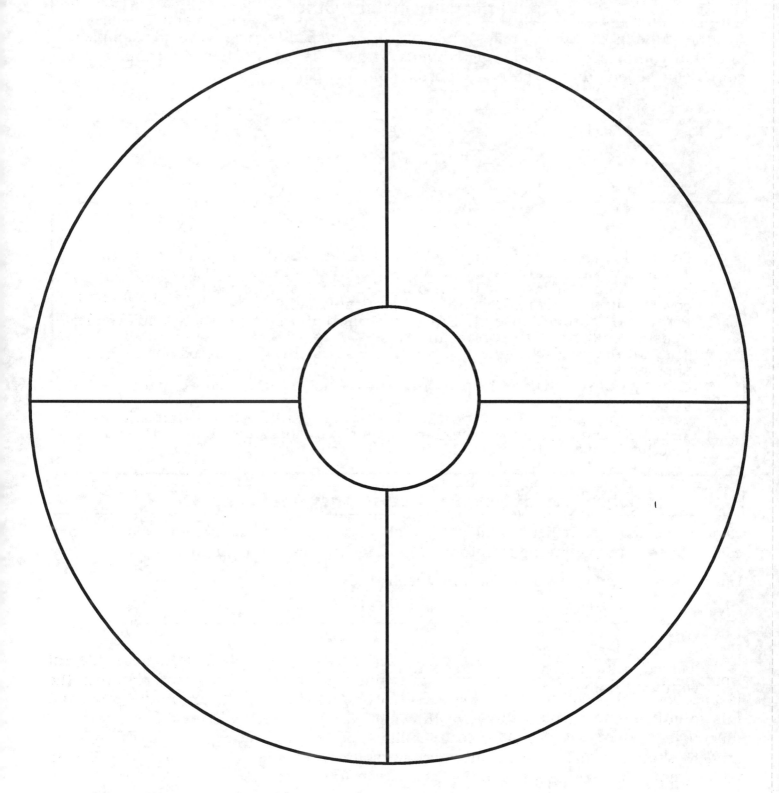

*See suggested activity, page 13.

What Is a Friend?

NOTE: This review activity has been divided into two parts. The first deals with concepts that have been introduced thus far, and the second deals with the remaining concept.

Part One

Cut butcher paper or white shelf paper into a 4 foot (1.2 meters) length, one per student. Fold paper into four equal sections.

To begin the review, have students write the first concept in the first section: What is a friend? Have each student draw a picture in that section to represent what a friend is to them. Discuss the concept. In the next section, have students write the second concept: It's fun to be with friends! Draw pictures and discuss, as with the first section. Repeat with the next concept: Friends help each other!

Part Two

When ready for the last section, write the following statement on the chalkboard and have students copy it in the remaining section: Friends can be different!

Have students think of a friend. Have them think of one way in which their friend is different from them, or they are different from their friend. Give them time to draw a picture in the last section that shows the difference. As they are doing this, walk around the room and talk to students about what they are drawing. If necessary, offer some ideas, such as differences in physical characteristics, abilities, or hobbies. When completed, let each student share his "difference." After all have shared, reinforce the idea that it is O.K. to be different from our friends, and it's O.K. for our friends to be different from us!

Before moving on to the next activity, have students work with partners to help each other memorize the four friendship concepts. Encourage them to remember these concepts while in the classroom, on the playground, in the lunchroom, at home, or playing with friends in the neighborhood!

If We Were All the Same

This activity is recommended to be used before reading any additional resources (p. 79) which emphasize the positive aspect of friends being different. Some excellent stories that meet this criteria are: *Rosie and Michael*; *How Joe the Bear and Sam the Mouse Got Together*; and *Ira Sleeps Over*.

To teach this lesson, make five copies of the following page. Color four of the five copies in a single color hue. (i.e., Color all the animals, people, trees, clouds, and other items with a red crayon on one sheet. Repeat with other copies using only a single color crayon.) Color the fifth copy with the appropriate color hues to look like a regular park scene. Shuffle the pictures and stack. Gather the students around you and ask them to observe the pictures you are going to show. Ask them to notice how each picture makes them feel, and to think about which picture looks the best. With no talking involved, show each picture for approximately 10 seconds. Go through the stack twice. Ask the students to react to what they saw. Most often the replies will be that the ones in which all the colors were the same "didn't look right," and the multi-colored scene will be the most pleasing. Use their reactions to convey that it is the same with our friends and friendships. If we were all the same, the world would be a very boring place. Because we are all so different, it makes being friends an exciting adventure!

Read the additional resources and evaluate as a class or in small groups, answering the following questions:

1. How were the friends alike?

2. How were the friends different?

3. Because the friends were different, how did they react to each other's differences?

4. Did any of the differences change during the story? Why?

5. If a friend is doing something that is different, but wrong (like cheating, stealing, lying), should we try to help them or let them stay "different"?

For an extension activity, allow students to illustrate an example of a way in which the story characters were different. Older students can also write a "book review" and share how friends can be different!

16

Park Scene

#274 Thematic Unit - Friendship

Best Friends

by Steven Kellogg

Summary

Best friends: we all have had at least one! Come and enjoy this delightful story of two best friends, Louise Jenkins and Kathy Cotski. Not only did they share an imaginary horse, Golden Silverwind, their desks at school, and the love of chocolate milk, but they learned the value of friendship by having to spend a summer apart. Great lessons in what being a friend really means are conveyed well through the excitement of the new neighbor's dog having puppies. Compromise, an essential ingredient to true friendship, helps to clear up a difficult situation when only one puppy is born!

The outline below is a suggested plan for using the various activities presented in this unit. You may adapt the ideas to meet specific needs in your classroom.

Sample Plan

Day I

- Sharing Our Emotions (p. 19)
- Read *Best Friends*
- Emotional Evaluation (p. 19)
- Framed Feelings (p. 29)
- My Best Friend (p. 30)
- Friendship Box (p. 20)

Day II

- Pick a Friend (p. 20)
- Friends Share Web (p. 20)
- Friendship Teams make Chocolate Milk Treat (p. 20)
- Friendship Hats Adventure (p. 21)
- Friendship Fractions (p. 43)
- Pen Pal Friends (p. 22)
- Create a Friendship Game (p. 20)
- Homework—Share it with a friend! (p. 56)

Day III

- Pick a New Friend—Share homework
- Cooperation Station (p. 23)
- Cooperation Chant (p. 28)
- Cooperation Quilt (p. 25)—Complete as a total class, discussing each square.

- Cooperative Cooking: "Sightless Sandwich" (p. 55)
- Cooperation Cards (p. 35)
- Cooperation Captions (p. 33)
- A Cooperating Concert (p. 52)

Day IV

- Pick a New Friend
- "I Care" Friendship Button (p. 19)
- Friends Care Chart (p. 26)
- Friends Care About Their Community (p. 37)
- Dog Bone Math (p. 46)
- Friendship Postcard (p. 34)
- A Friendly Flower Experiment (p. 47)
- I Am a Friend Mobile (p. 38)

Day V

- Culminating Activity— A FRIENDSHIP FAIR (pp. 59–60)

    Heart to Heart

    Friendship Band

    Friendship Necklace

    Friendship 500

    Friendship Read-a-thon

Overview of Activities

SETTING THE STAGE

1. Ask students to share how it makes them feel to be with their friends. Ask them to tell you how it makes them feel when a friend says: "You are nice." (happy); "I'm going to tell the teacher on you!" (angry); "I got a new bike and you didn't." (jealous); "You are my best friend." (special). Explain that these feelings are called emotions.

2. Friends share feelings (emotions). On a large sheet of white butcher paper write the word "Emotions" in bold letters. Have the students brainstorm as many "emotion" words as they can. List them on the butcher paper with a black marker.

    Show the cover of *Best Friends*. Share that the two main characters of the story are Louise and Kathy. They are best friends. Ask the class to look at their emotions chart. Since the girls are best friends, what emotions will they experience in the story? Use a red marker to place a red star next to the hypothesized emotions.

3. Make "I Care" Friendship Buttons to wear during the friendship activities. To make the buttons, copy the button pattern (p. 71) onto tagboard. Give one to each student and allow him/her to draw in his/her own face. Glue or tape a safety pin to the back of the cut-out tagboard button. Let dry. (Alternative method: Copy pattern onto white paper. After students draw themselves, cut out around edge and use in a standard button-making machine.)

ENJOYING THE BOOK

1. Do this emotional evaluation activity after completing Setting the Stage-2 and reading the story. Reread the story slowly. Have students stop you when the girls are showing emotions. Each time an emotion is identified, look back at the emotions chart. If it appears on the chart, circle it with red marker. If it is an emotion that does not appear on the chart, add it with the red marker. When the story review is complete, look back at the chart to study the emotions of these two "best friends." (It will show that best friends are not always "buddy, buddy," but can sometimes have feelings of anger, jealousy, envy, and other strong emotions, and still be good friends.) Ask them why they believe this can be true. Remind them of the three rules they learned when reading *Friends* (p. 12).

Overview of Activities *(cont.)*

2. "Pick a Friend" Activity—Place all the names of your students onto small strips of paper. Place in a container labeled "Friendship Teams." Each day, for days 2, 3, and 4 have students take turns picking out a name to form a Friendship Team. The "team" will remain together while participating and completing the activities for that day. Remember, each day the students pick out a new teammate. (After all of the strips are selected, simply place them back into the container so they will be ready for the next day.)

3. Create a "Friends Share" web. Have students brainstorm all of the ways that they share with their friends. Remind them that a friend can be a classmate, family member, neighbor, or even an animal.

    FRIENDS SHARE

4. Provide each friendship team with the supplies and ingredients to make a glass of chocolate milk. Ask the students what Kathy and Louise's favorite drink is! Have teams make their glass of chocolate milk, adding two straws to the glass as a finishing touch! Reread the story *Best Friends* while the teams sip their chocolate milk. After reading, use the web to compare how the characters in the story shared with the ways in which the students said they share. For an extension, make a Venn diagram showing the ways in which the class shares the same and differently from the story's characters.

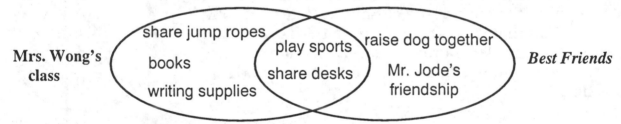

Mrs. Wong's class — share jump ropes, books, writing supplies — play sports, share desks — raise dog together, Mr. Jode's friendship — **Best Friends**

EXTENDING THE BOOK

1. Following the same guidelines as in Create a Game (p. 41), have students create games that review various skills being introduced or reviewed in your classroom.

2. Friends care about their community. This is an important statement, and young children need to realize that they are part of a community. They can learn to be community friends. Some possible activities to fulfill this experience are: visiting a senior citizens home and making cards or gifts for the residents; going to an animal shelter to help brush the animals and clean out the pens; cleaning up a local park; collecting newspapers or pop can tops to raise money for medical research.

3. Have students create a friendship box by covering a shoebox with colorful contact paper. Have students fill their boxes with treasures from home and school. Have each student share his/her box with the class in an oral report format. Display boxes for all to view!

Friendship Hats

Louise and Kathy enjoyed pretending that their neighborhood was a magical place, full of fun and adventure!

Have each friendship team make a pair of friendship hats (directions below). After the hats have been created and placed on their heads, allow the teams to do one or more of the suggested activities!

Directions:

1. Cut blue butcher paper to the dimensions shown, one per student.

2. Provide crayons, markers, colored chalk, glitter, and glue. Have students decorate their hats.

3. To assemble hats, have one team member "curl" the pattern to form a cone, while the other member uses transparent tape along the edge to hold the cone-shaped hat together.

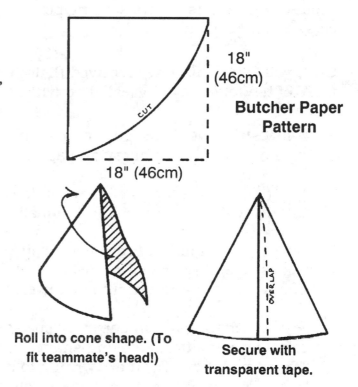

Butcher Paper Pattern

18" (46cm)

18" (46cm)

CUT

Roll into cone shape. (To fit teammate's head!)

Secure with transparent tape.

OVERLAP

Activities:

1. Pretend you are riding Golden Silverwind through your school. What would the school area turn into in your imagination?

2. Pretend that the friendship hats could let you go anywhere in the world (without flying in a plane!). Where would you go? What would you see? What would you do there?

3. Provide a large sheet of butcher paper. Allow teams to draw their own fantasy land using lots of details like Steven Kellogg did when he illustrated his book.

4. Pretend that it is dark outside and you and your teammate have to walk home. From what monsters or other scary things will your friendship hats keep you safe?

5. Mr. Jode wished that Kathy's hat had magic powers to find homes for all of Sarah's new puppies. If the friendship team's hats had special magic powers to help someone in need, who would it be and how would they help that person?

Pen Pal Friends

Writing to a pen pal provides the opportunity for students to gain knowledge and insight about how students live, learn, and play in other states, provinces, or countries!

There are many different ways to obtain pen pals for your class. You can simply work with another teacher in your school or district. If you have a student who has entered your class from another state or country, his or her former teacher may be an excellent resource. Check teacher magazines. They often offer some type of reader exchange that lists others seeking pen pals or allows you to solicit a group for your class to correspond with.

Once your students have received their pen pal names, complete and send one or more of the following suggested activities:

1. Allow students to design their own pen pal stationery to use when writing to their pals or use the stationery on page 11.

2. Enclose various forms of artwork done by the students. Note: Art must be relatively flat to get through the mail.

3. Make a chain letter. Provide wide strips of paper for each student. Let them write a message to their pen pal. Staple all of the strips into connected loops to form a chain. Flatten and put into an envelope.

4. Provide shape-pattem paper for special occasions. Example: pumpkin-shaped for a Halloween letter; stocking-shaped for a Christmas letter; heart-shaped for a Valentine letter. If you are writing to pals in a different country, this would be a good opportunity to describe our holiday customs.

    No matter which activity the students are doing, encourage them to follow these steps when writing to their pen pals. Ask the corresponding class's teacher to ask his/her students to do the same.

    - **Answer any questions asked.**
    - **Ask a new question about your pen pal.**
    - **Tell your pen pal something new about yourself.**
    - **Share a recent experience that happened to you at home or at school.**

Note: Writing to pen pals is a good time to review the parts of a letter!

Cooperation Station

Helping each other learn or complete a project.

Write the definition of cooperation on chart paper. Discuss the meaning with the students. Ask, for example, how Kathy and Louise cooperated in the story *Best Friends*. Pose the following question:

If we cooperate, can we learn faster or finish projects quicker?

On chart paper have the students write their names under their hypothesized choice to the posed question. Then proceed with the following activity to discover the correct answer.

Explain that you want the class to create Love Coupons (p. 24) to be used for an upcoming activity. Tell them that you are going to have some of the students assemble the coupons individually, while a group of students will form a "cooperation station" and put the coupons together in an assembly-line fashion. Emphasize that the cooperation station will have to cooperate to complete the making of their coupons!

If we cooperate, can we learn faster or finish projects quicker?		
YES		NO
Susan	Sam	Ron
Jim	Tom	Mary
Marvin	Trisha	Iona

Assign a student to each cooperation station job listed below. Create the assembly-line layout in the classroom. When a student is assigned a job, he is to sit in the appropriate area.

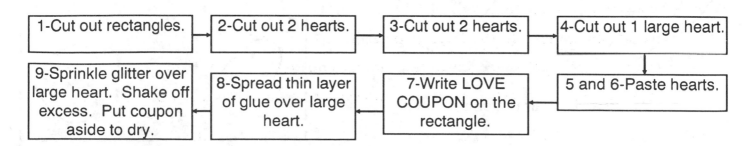

1-Cut out rectangles. → 2-Cut out 2 hearts. → 3-Cut out 2 hearts. → 4-Cut out 1 large heart.

9-Sprinkle glitter over large heart. Shake off excess. Put coupon aside to dry. ← 8-Spread thin layer of glue over large heart. ← 7-Write LOVE COUPON on the rectangle. ← 5 and 6-Paste hearts.

Cooperation Station *(cont.)*

Materials:

White construction paper (which will be cut by station 1 into 5" X 3"/13cm X 8cm rectangles); scissors for stations 1-4; red construction paper containing heart patterns, below—small hearts for stations 2,3/large hearts for station 4; paste—stations 5,6; thin-tipped black felt pens—station 7; glue—station 8; glitter—station 9.

Directions:

Lay out the necessary materials at each station area. Provide the same materials for each individual student, who will be making the Love Coupons with no help from classmates. Set a timer for five or ten minutes and let the cooperation station and individual coupon makers begin. At the end of the designated time, compare how many coupons were completed by the cooperation station team compared to those students working individually. Look back at the hypothesized question. The cooperation station activity should have proven that when we do work together to help complete a project or learn, we can get more accomplished! Collect finished coupons to be used for a later activity. Make sure there are at least 2 coupons per student.

Remember: Supplies will also be needed by each individual student who will be assembling Love Coupons without help!

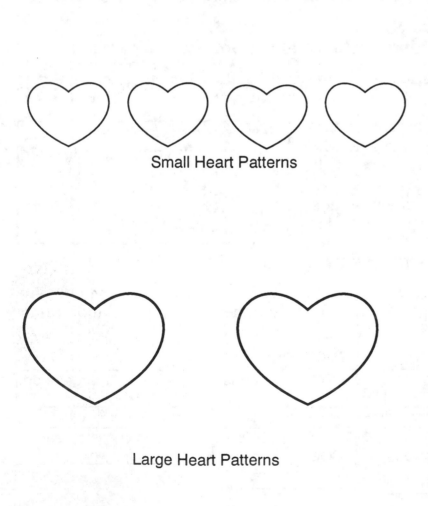

Small Heart Patterns

Large Heart Patterns

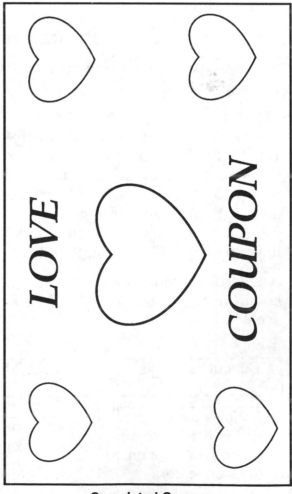

Completed Coupon

Cooperation Quilt

Read each square. Use **red** to color the examples of friends cooperating. Use **blue** to color examples of friends not cooperating.

fighting for a jump rope	sharing a cookie	grabbing a book a friend is reading	stirring and baking homemade cookies with a friend
helping a friend learn to ride a bike	stealing a friend's pencil	cleaning the bathroom for your mom or dad	hitting your sister or brother
telling friends they can't be on your team	helping sound out the hard words for a friend	making noises so your teacher can not be heard	lending an eraser to a classmate
untangling a set of earphones at a listening center	throwing food at a classmate in the lunchroom	babysitting a younger brother or sister	calling a classmate a mean name
poking someone in line with a pencil	feeding your dog or cat so they stay healthy	hiding a friend's homework	helping a friend know how to spell a word

Challenge: Make a life-size cooperation quilt by drawing a picture of your favorite things on 8 1/2" X 12" (20 cm x 30 cm) construction paper. Place everyone's picture in a quilt pattern on the wall. Can you think of a good title for your class quilt?

Friends Care Chart

Even though Kathy got angry and jealous of her best friend, Louise, she still cared about her. It is important to care about our friends. We can take care of friends in various ways. On large paper, draw a chart (as shown below) including the headings, but not the examples (These are given as a teacher reference). Ask the students to listen carefully as you reread the story. When they think that someone in the story is caring, they are to give you a signal (raising hand, whistling, thumbs-up, clapping). Discuss the student's observations, deciding on who is being the friend, with whom they are being a friend, how they are being a friend, and why they are being a friend. As this information is contributed, list it on the chart paper under the correct heading. Continue with the remainder of the story. Hand out the Friends Care Chart (p. 27) and have students think about who they care about. Let them fill out their chart on their own, or with an adult helping to write responses. Share charts as a total group or in small group settings. Collect and bind finished charts with a construction paper cover and back to form a "We Care" book. Place in a reading area for all to read.

Hand out two love coupons (p. 24) per student to give to a friend to show they love and care about them!

WHO IS BEING A FRIEND?	TO WHOM IS SHE/HE BEING A FRIEND?	HOW IS SHE/HE BEING A FRIEND?	WHY IS SHE/HE BEING A FRIEND?
Kathy	Louise	nurses her with chocolate milk	she has a contagious disease
Louise	Kathy	wrote her a postcard	wants to tell her she missed her
Kathy	Mr. Jode	asks him to a cookout	we should be good neighbors
Louise	Kathy	brought her a present	because she liked her
Louise's Mother	Louise	reserves a puppy	because she loved her
Louise and Kathy	Mr. Jode	helps him deliver Sarah's puppies	wanted to help if he needed it
Mr. Jode	Louise and Kathy	will build Golden Silverwind's house	wanted to help them share the puppy
Louise and Kathy	to each other	they are going to raise Sarah's puppy, Golden Silverwind, together	because they are friends and they know how to Cooperate!

26

Friends Care Chart

Hi, my name is _____ and I care about...

WHO?	HOW?	WHY?

Poetry

Friends Are Fun Acrostic

An acrostic poem is a wonderful writing experience that encourages students to expand their vocabulary. As a class, write a sample acrostic on the board. Then, just for "fun," allow the students to sit anywhere in the room to write their own acrostic. Have students share their poems.

Display the poems in the hallway for other school friends to enjoy!

Friends
Really are   Ask to   For
Incredible   Read   Unforgettable
Especially   Everyday   New friendship
New next   fun!
Door
Schoolmates

A "Round" of Song

A song is often written in rhyming form. Teach the simple song below (set to the tune of "Row, Row, Row Your Boat"). After students become familiar with the lyrics, divide the class into two teams. Teach the song as a round (second team begins singing after the first team finishes the first line). If students enjoy a two-part round, divide teams again and try a four-part friendship sing-a-thon!

Love, love, love your friends,
Different as they seem.
Playing, laughing, joking, helping,
True friends are in our dreams!

Cooperation Chant

This cooperation chant has a strong rhythm. After students learn the words, they can say the chant while "marching" to the lunch room, bus, or special activity!

1. We are friends, yes we are,

   Cooperation is our star!

   To the left and to the right,

   We will help you become bright!

2. We are friends, yes we are,

   Cooperation is our star!

   To the sky and to the ground,

   We will praise you all around!

3. We are friends, yes we are,

   Cooperation is our star!

   To the East and to the West,

   Cooperating is the BEST!

28

Writing Activities

Note to Teacher: To help students reach their maximum writing potential, enlist the help of volunteers or aides during the language experiences.

My Friends Book

After discussing the concept of "friendship," a "My Friends" book will give your students an opportunity to tell about their friends in a written form. Use the writing sheet (p. 31) and reproduce five or six per student. Hand out and allow students to complete. When finished, give each student two sheets of colored construction paper for a cover and back page. Allow them to decorate the cover as desired, being sure to include the title "My Friends." Have the class share their books orally, then place in a reading area for all to enjoy!

"I Can Be Different" Accordion Book

To make an accordion book, fold four 12" X 18" pieces of colored paper in half. Tape "middle" edges to form accordion pages. Completed books can be folded for easy storage. To complete the "I Can Be Different" accordion book, have students write sentences as shown below, then illustrate them. For younger students, write the text they recite and allow them to illustrate.

Framed Feelings

Use the sheet on page 32. Explain to the class that you want them to draw a picture in the frame showing how they can make a friend feel happy today. After they draw the picture, tell them to write a sentence or two to explain their drawing. Display the framed feelings in the hallway or classroom with the title, "We've Been Framed!"

Be a Friend

Be a Friend Poster

The definition of a poster, according to Webster's Dictionary, is "a large public advertisement or notice posted publicly." Discuss this meaning with your students. Explain that you are going to "hire" them to create a poster for a school "ad campaign." The campaign slogan is "How to Be a Friend." Provide each student with a large piece of tagboard or butcher paper. Review ways in which friends can help each other by looking at the completed friendship wheels (p. 13). Provide markers, crayons, chalk, and/or paints for students to create their posters. Display the posters in "public view" by placing them in the hallways, library, lunchroom, and bathrooms around school. Note: You can form poster teams of 3 or 4 to create a single poster.

My Best Friend

Materials: Large sheets of construction or butcher paper; markers; yarn; glitter; glue

A best friend is somebody special. Have students create a special "body" that tells everyone why a friend is a **best** friend. Make a sample (similar to the one at right) to show your students who your best friend is. Provide large sheets of construction paper or butcher paper for the students to use to cut and paste to form their friends' bodies. Offer crayons, markers, glitter, yarn, and other craft supplies to add the details to their friends' faces. Have the students write the facts about their best friends on the body parts. Let students share their best friends. Display the friends for all to see...and read!

My Friend

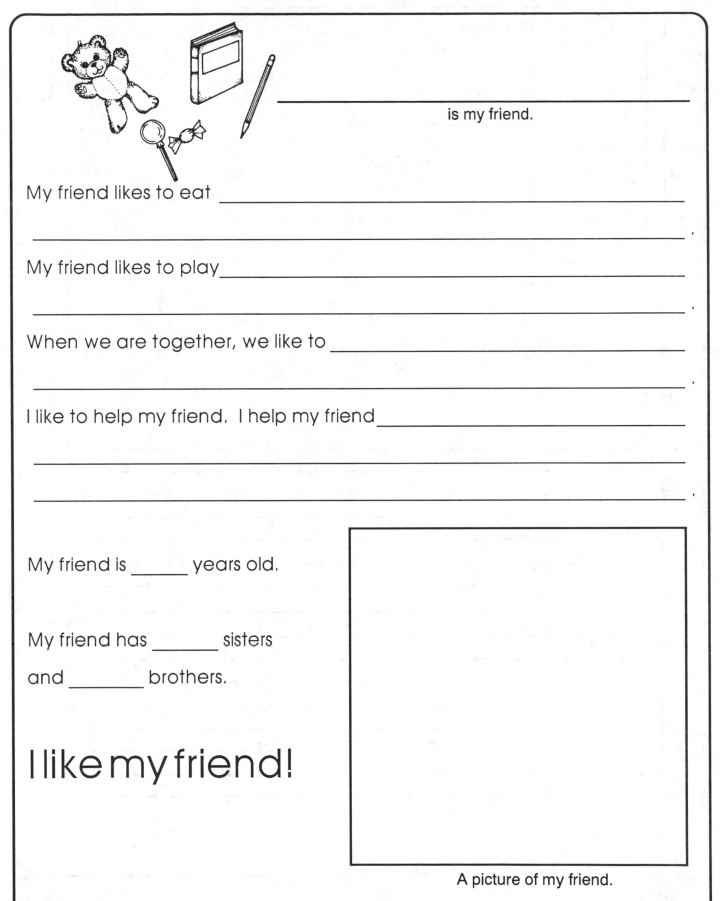

_____ is my friend.

My friend likes to eat _____

_____ .

My friend likes to play _____

_____ .

When we are together, we like to _____

_____ .

I like to help my friend. I help my friend _____

_____

_____ .

My friend is _____ years old.

My friend has _____ sisters

and _____ brothers.

I like my friend!

A picture of my friend.

By:

32

Cooperation Captions

Write what the characters say to show that they are cooperating.

Friendship Postcard

1. Write a postcard to a friend.

2. Pretend you are on a trip. Tell your friend what you have been doing.

3. After writing your postcard, cut out and illustrate the other side with a picture of you and your family on your trip. Share your postcard with the friend you are writing to!

Dear _____,

_____

_____

_____

_____

_____

Love, your friend,

_____

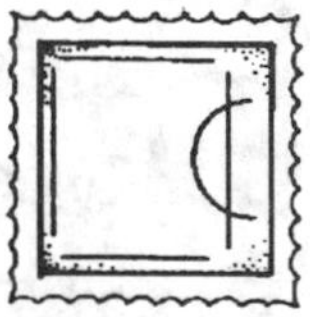

To:

_____

_____

_____

_____

For fun: Use a regular 5" X 7" color photo of you on a trip. Turn the back into a real postcard. Add a stamp and mail it to a friend!

Cooperation Cards

Divide the class into teams of four or five. Provide each team with two or three cooperation cards (reproduced from pages 35 and 36, and cut along solid lines). Give each team five minutes to cooperate and discuss how they would work together to solve the problem on each card. Share in whole group.

Your team is lost in the desert with one blanket, one bag of fruit, and 1 canteen of water. How will you share?

A mom and dad will pay your team $5.00 to clean the back yard. Who will do what jobs?

Your team needs to plan a nice surprise party for a friend. What will the party be like?

Your teacher wants to make up a play. Who will the characters be? What jobs will need to be done?

Your team is going to visit a Senior Home. How can you make the people there happy?

Your team is going to make chocolate chip cookies. Who will be responsible for what job?

     #274 Thematic Unit - Friendship

Cooperation Cards *(cont.)*

Reproduce. Cut along solid lines.

Your team is at recess. What games can you play so that everyone will be a winner?

Your teacher wants your team to make a dinosaur mural. Who will draw what?

There is a new student in your class. How can you become friends with him or her?

Your team is watching cartoons. How can everyone get to see what they want?

Your team is going on a picnic in the park. What will each person bring?

A friend's dad is planting a vegetable garden. How can your team help?

RADISHES   BEANS   CARROTS

36

Friends Care About Their Community

What is a friend? What is a community? Review what it means to be a good friend. Discuss the meaning of a community. Have students brainstorm how they can be a help to their community.

FRIEND
A person who cares and helps.

COMMUNITY
Any group living in the same area.

Listed below are some ways in which your class can be a help to the community. Choose one or more of the following. (Note: One of the activities will need to be chosen for use in the Friendship 500, a part of the Friendship Fair culminating activity.)

Saving old newspapers or aluminum products for such organizations as crisis centers, hospital drives, medical needs, community food banks

Saving used clothing and articles for homeless shelters, handicapped rehabilitation programs, medical drives, elderly homes, public assistance leagues

Adopting a group or organization to spend time with, or raising money for elderly homes, homeless shelters, after-school low-income programs, UNICEF or other world-wide relief organizations

Caring about the nature of our communities by collecting trash in the neighborhood parks, telling people not to litter through a poster campaign, writing letters to political officials about nature concerns in your city, state, province, or country

I Am a Friend Mobile

Materials: Patterns (pages 39-40); tagboard or stiff paper; hole punch; yarn; scissors; markers or crayons

Directions: Reproduce the patterns onto tagboard or another stiff paper product. Students read their mobile pieces and add the appropriate names. They complete the project by illustrating, cutting out, and putting it together. To assemble the mobile, punch holes through the black dots and string colored yarn through them to create the mobile effect. For added fun, students can add a second animal, family member, friend, and community organization to the backs of the four circles.

I Am a Friend Mobile (cont.)

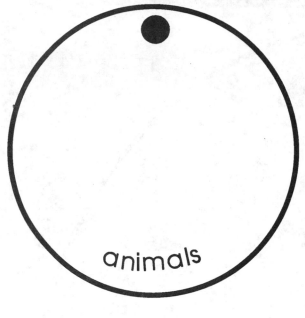

animals

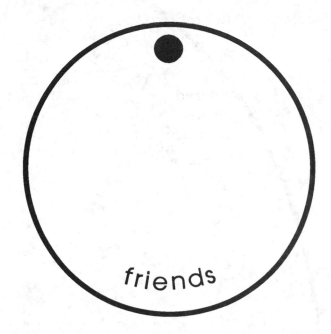

friends

family

community

*See page 38 for suggested activity.

I Am a Friend Mobile *(cont.)*

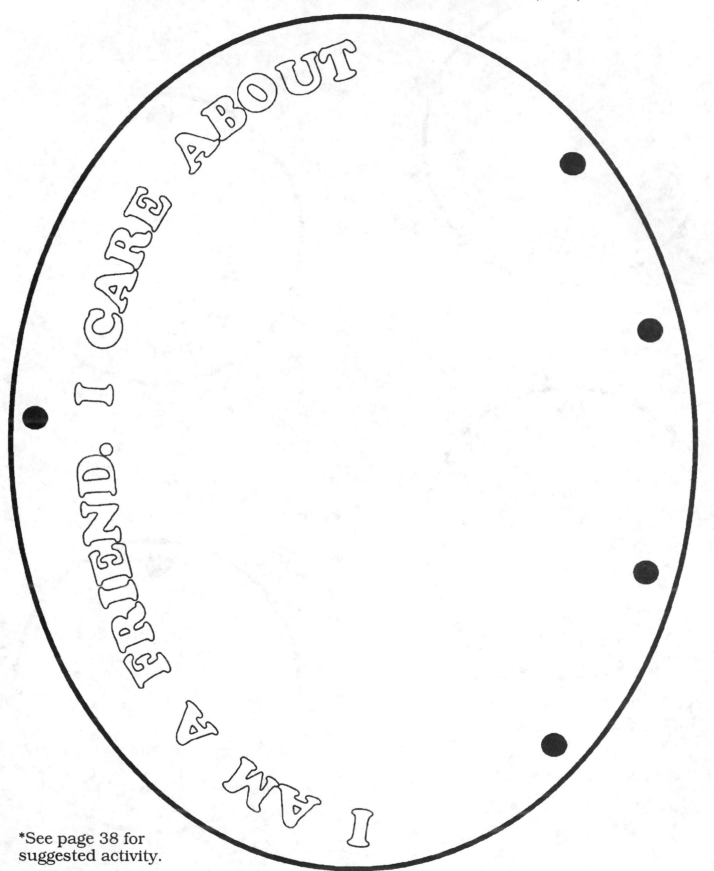

I AM A FRIEND. I CARE ABOUT

*See page 38 for
suggested activity.

40

Friendly Math Activities

Create a Game

Students play a lot of games at home and at school. They are actually game experts! Let them put some of their expert energy into creating their own math games! These games can be gameboards, outdoor, indoor, manipulative, or other varieties of games. Try not to stifle the student's creativity by setting limits on how the game should be created. The only two rules should be: math skills being learned or reviewed must be incorporated, and the game should be fair and fun! Provide markers, paper, dice, counters, beans, spinners, small bowls, and other manipulatives to spark their creativity. Divide the class into teams of four or five to create a game. After games are constructed, allow each team to show how its game is played. Let students rotate and try the other games. When done with the math activity, put the games in a Friendly Math Center for free time use!

Math Facts Friendly Review

Materials: Pattern reproduced from page 42; tagboard or stiff paper; hole punch; craft sticks; stapler; golf tees

Use the pattern and follow the directions on page 42 to create math fact review cards. Use golf tees for the answering instrument (this works much better than pencils which leave marks!) Divide the class into friendly teams of two. Provide each team with a different math fact review card. Have each member take turns completing the card (see page 42 for directions). When the problem-solver is finished with the card, the two players switch jobs. When each team is done with its card, the teams rotate and receive a new card. Proceed in the same manner until each team has had all of the math skill review cards. Place cards in the math center area for use during free time.

Math Facts Friendly Review Card

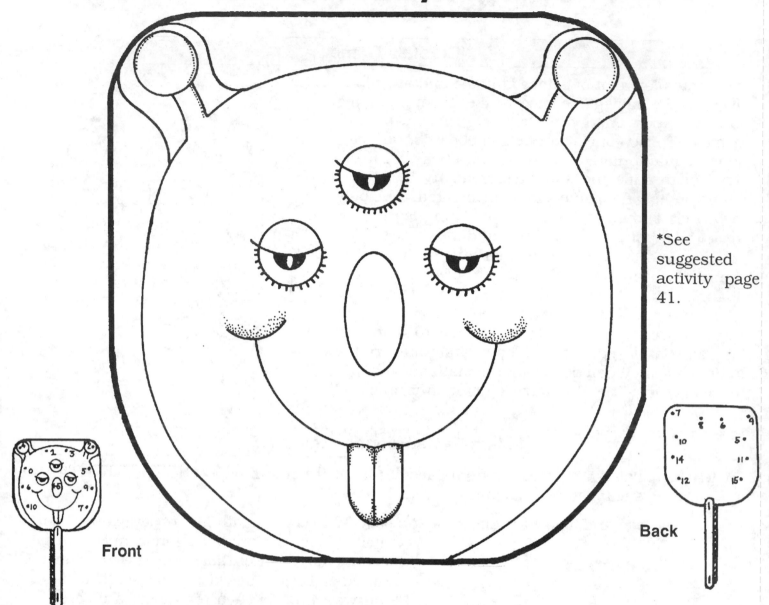

*See suggested activity page 41.

Front

Back

Directions: Make as many friendly math Martians as you will need. Glue onto heavy tagboard for durability; color; cut out. In the center oval, write an operation sign (+, -, x, ÷) and the number you want to review. Punch holes along perimeter with hole punch. Write a different number next to each hole. Turn Martian over and write answers to the problems next to the proper hole. Turn Martian over and write answers to the problems next to the proper hole. Laminate and cut out. Staple two craft sticks together to the bottom of each Martian, placing one stick on either side of the Martian.

To Play: One child faces the front of the Martian, while another child faces the back. The child facing the front puts a golf tee through a hole next to a number and says the problem aloud. (In the diagram, for example, five will be added to each number. If the child puts the tee in the three, he would say, "Five plus three equals eight.") The child facing the back of the Martian checks the answers. After all problems have been computed, the children trade places.

Friendship Fractions

A unit on friendship provides an ideal time to introduce the concept of fractions! Follow the lessons below to create exciting concrete experiences:

Rules:	1/2	one-half means one out of two equal parts
	1/3	one-third means one out of three equal parts
	1/4	one-fourth means one out of four equal parts

Lesson 1: Draw a circle on the chalkboard; add a wavy line around the edge to give the appearance of a pizza pie crust. Tell the class that you and (choose a student's name) went to have a pizza. You are going to eat half and so is ____. "Cut" the pizza with a different color chalk, but do not cut it into equal halves. State that you are going to eat the bigger part, while _____ gets the smaller part. Ask the class if this is fair. You'll get a resounding, "NO!" Ask why. When students say that you are getting more, restate it by saying you and ____ are not getting equal parts.

Activity 1: Using dry erase boards or sheets of white paper, ask students to draw their own pizza. Draw another pizza on the board and divide it in half equally with a vertical line. Write 1/2 in one section of the pizza and say, "I am going to eat one of the two equal parts." Repeat for the other half, replacing the student's name with yours. Ask the students to "cut" their pizza into two equal parts. Have students evaluate their halves. If not equal, ask them to try and "cut" it again. When all pizzas have been cut equally, have the students write 1/2 in one section while stating the same type of sentence you modeled. Repeat with the other side having them replace their name with a friend's name. Repeat the activity, this time cutting the pizzas with a horizontal line through the middle. For further reinforcement, have students shade 1/2 of the pizza.

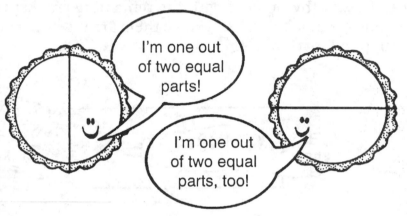

I'm one out of two equal parts!

I'm one out of two equal parts, too!

Lesson 2: Review the concept of 1/2. Draw a rectangle (to represent a cracker) on the chalkboard. Explain that you want to share this cracker with yourself and three other students. Ask three students to come to the chalkboard. Divide the cracker into four **unequal** parts. Point to each part that you and the students will get, making sure that you get the largest part. Ask them if they think you are being fair. Again, you'll get a resounding, "NO!" Ask why. This time they should be able to tell you it is because the cracker has not been divided into equal parts. Draw another rectangular-shaped cracker on the board and divide it into four **equal** parts.

(continued on next page.)

Friendship Fractions *(cont.)*

Ask if the students think they will be getting equal parts now! Let the students return to their seats. Write 1/4 in the first section. State that you are going to be eating one out of four equal parts. Repeat with remaining sections, replacing student's names with yours. Show other examples of four equal parts:

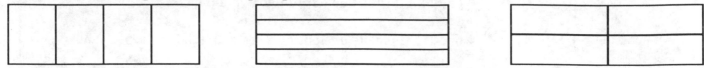

Activity 2: Divide the class into teams of four. Give each team four large graham crackers (the type where you can see the lines that divide the cracker into four sections) and a small tube of ready-made frosting. Have the teams notice that they have four **whole** crackers. Into how many sections is each cracker divided? Are the sections equal? To find out, carefully divide **one** of the crackers along the perforations. Give each team member one of these sections. Have them stack the four sections to see if they are equal. Then, have the team members lay their sections on top of one of the whole crackers to see if the parts form a whole. Once it has been determined that each child does have one of four equal parts of a whole, have the students use the frosting to label their parts with the fraction, 1/4. Repeat the process with the remaining crackers until each student has four cracker sections, each labeled 1/4. Have them arrange their sections as a whole cracker and enjoy them, one-fourth at a time.

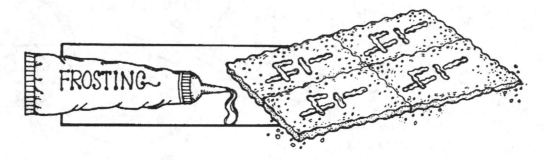

Lesson 3: This lesson covers the concept of 1/3. This fraction can be a little more tricky to teach. Just remember to emphasize equal parts. Review the concepts of 1/2 and 1/4. Draw a square on the chalkboard. Pretend the square is a cookie and you want to share it with two other students. Divide unequally, then equally. Repeat the process with a triangular-shaped "cookie" stating that you will be eating one out of three equal parts.

Activity 3: Divide the class into teams of three. Provide each team with three soft round chocolate chip cookies and small plastic knife. Have each team member cut his cookie into three equal parts.

Students then trade one out of three equal parts three times so that they end up with a whole cookie again. Let everyone enjoy their triple good chocolate chip treat!

Review or Test Time: Use the worksheet on page 45 to determine which students have mastered the concepts of 1/2, 1/3, and 1/4.

Friendly Fractions

1. Color each 1/2 brown.   2. Color each 1/3 yellow.
3. Color each 1/4 red.

Dog Bone Math

To practice oral addition and subtraction problems, have each student make her own dog bone math game. Provide the pieces below (reproduced onto tagboard) and a small self-sealing plastic bag (for storing). After students color and cut out pieces, give a few examples of how to use the game pieces. Allow students to play "solitaire" or with partners!

Examples:

"There are three bones in the dog dish. Mary added three more. How many bones are in the dish in all?"

"I put eight bones in the dog dish. My dog, Golden Silverwind, ate five bones. How many bones are left in the bowl?"

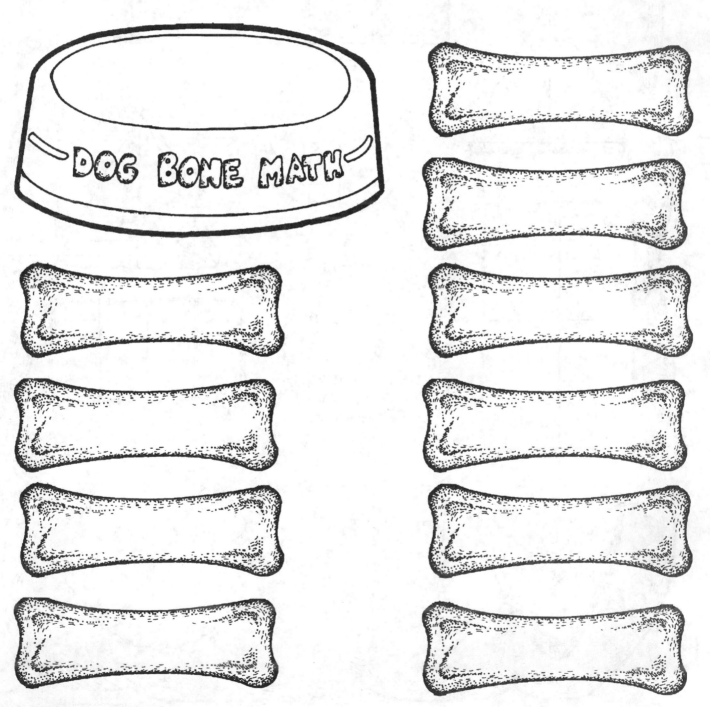

46

Friendly Science Experiments

How Are We Different?

Materials: Rulers; measuring tapes; watches or clock with a second hand

Directions:

Use page 48 to complete this science experiment. Provide each student with a separate sheet. Review pulse taking. (With your right hand palm up, place the index and middle fingers of your left hand flat on the area of your wrist below the thumb. Wait until you find a steady pulse. Using a second hand to time yourself, count the number of beats you feel in sixty seconds.) Simply follow the directions on the page and let the class see how they are different.

Note: To simplify the measuring, divide the class into teams of three and allow them to measure, and check the pulse of each other.

A Friendly Flower

Materials: One white carnation per team; two glasses of water; knife; food coloring

Directions:

Students will love the "results" of this experiment! Divide the class into friendship teams of two. Provide each team with one white carnation (often flower stores or outlets will donate or reduce the cost of the carnations) and the worksheet on page 49. Have students decide on their hypothesis and proceed with the experiment. (Adult helpers may be needed to assist friendship teams in splitting their stem properly.) After the students have arrived at their conclusion, let them decide on whom they can bestow their special carnation to show that they care!

How Are We Different?

Our bodies are growing every day. Friends grow and change at different rates. Find out ways that you are the same or different from your friends.

Hypothesis

*Check one:

_____ I am different from my friends in many ways.

_____ I am the same as my friends.

Procedure

Fill in the chart after using the correct measuring method.

What to Measure . . .	My Name _____	Friend One _____	Friend Two _____	Measuring Method
Measure your arm from elbow to fingertips.				
Measure your body from your head to your heel.				
Take your pulse. How many times does it beat in one minute?				
Measure the length of your foot from your heel to your toes.				

Results

*Use your chart to fill in blanks.

My arm is longer than _____. My arm is shorter than _____ .

I am taller than _____. I am shorter than _____ .

My heart beats faster than _____. My heart beats slower than_____ .

My foot is longer than_____. My foot is shorter than _____ .

Conclusion

*Circle the correct response.

1. **My friends and I are different.**   2. **My friends and I are the same.**

A Friendly Flower

Hypothesis

Circle your choice.

1. Flowers "drink" water through their stems to nourish their petals.

2. Flowers nourish their petals with the invisible water in the air.

Procedure

1. Cut the stem of your flower. Be careful and do not cut completely apart!

2. Fill the two glasses with water. Decide the two colors you will use to color the glasses of water.

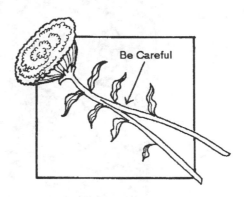

_____ my color	_____ my friend's color

3. Put a small amount of the correct food coloring in the glasses.

4. Carefully place 1/2 of the stem in one glass and the other 1/2 of the stem in the other glass.

5. Let your flower sit overnight.

6. Observe your flower. What do you see?

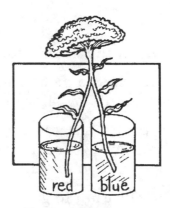

Results

Here is what our flower looked like the next day:

Conclusion

Circle your answer.

My hypothesis was

correct   incorrect

To show we care, we are going to give our friendly flower to:

_____

Friends Across the Globe

Listed below are a variety of activities that you can do to expand your students' understanding of the world around them:

1. Show the class a globe with your location labeled. Introduce the various countries and continents by showing pictures of children from those places.

2. Gather poster-size pictures of children from other countries and display on a bulletin board. As each country is discussed, share facts about how the children there live and go to school. Enjoy a simple food from that country.

3. Ask the librarian to gather a large assortment of books about the lives of friends around the globe.

4. Show 16 mm films or video tapes, available through your public library, which provide information on the lifestyles of children from other lands.

5. Contact a non-profit, multi-cultural organization to come and speak to your students. Don't forget to write them a thank you letter!

6. Learn dances or songs from various countries.

7. If students are old enough, divide into friendship learning teams and assign each team a country. The students research their country's way of life and report back to the class by presenting an oral report and posters created by the team.

8. After learning about children in other lands, have the students write a class Big Book about the different cultures. Provide pictures of the children from the various locations taught for reference as students illustrate their Big Book.

50

Friends Across the Wall

This art activity will show that our classmates are our friends. Review what a friend is. Illustrate those concepts with examples of how the class acts as friends towards one another. Place all of the class's names into a container. Have each student select someone else's name and follow the procedure below:

Materials: 8 1/2" x 11" paper; crayons; scissors; markers or pencils; stapler or tape

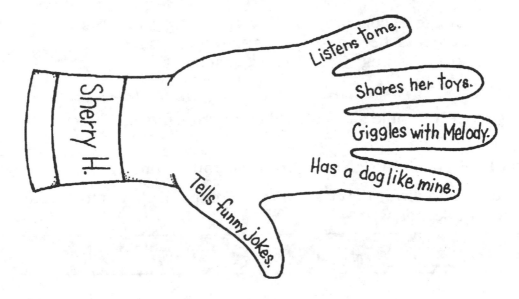

Procedure:

1. Think of ways the person whose name was drawn shows that he/she is a friend to you or someone else in the room.

2. On a sheet of 8 1/2" X 11" paper, outline your hand with a pencil.

3. Retrace your hand shape with a brown crayon.

4. Cut out carefully.

5. Draw a bracelet on your paper wrist and put the name you drew on it.

6. On each finger write a way in which your classmate is a friend.

7. Make a chain of all the hands across the wall, either in your classroom or down the hall!

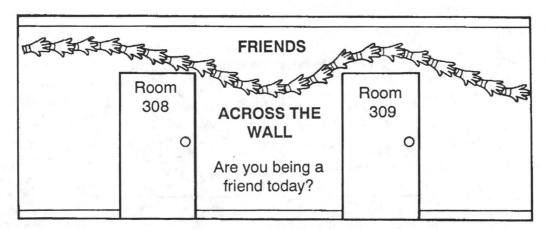

A Cooperating Concert

Conductor

The definition of an orchestra is a group of people playing music together by cooperating.

The orchestra puts on a concert.

Create a cooperation concert by having your students become the musicians and take turns leading as the concert conductor!

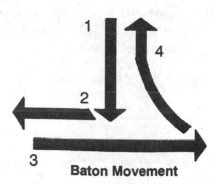

Baton Movement

The musicians are responsible for playing their instruments and cooperating with the conductor.

The conductor is responsible for leading the cooperating concert.

To create your orchestra divide the class into four groups. Each group will play instruments from one of the four sections:

Percussion	Woodwinds	Brass	Strings
cymbal drum triangle sticks xylophone	flute kazoo recorder whistle	horn trumpet bugle	autoharp guitar ukulele violin
Note: If students can not play a real instrument, substitute with home-made or toy versions!			

Have students sit in chairs or on the floor according to the diagram below. Explain that they are not to play unless the conductor signals to them. This is how the orchestra cooperates with each other and the conductor.

Conductor Signals:

1. Taps desk with baton —orchestra becomes quiet.
2. Raises both arms in the air —orchestra gets ready to play.

The conductor has four signals to tell his orchestra what to do. They are all done with his hands. Take turns being the conductor!

3. Points with one hand to a particular section—that section begins to play.
4. Keeps everyone on the same beat by completing baton movement (above) with other hand.

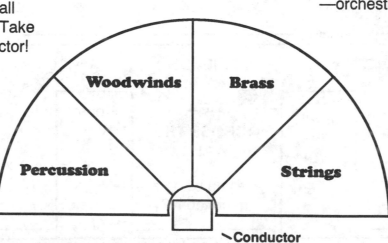

Friendship Exercise Course

To complete the Friendship Exercise Course divide the class into friendship teams of two. When a team has completed the course, have a cool treat waiting to celebrate their success!

To set up course activities, follow diagram below. Enlist adult help to stand as monitors throughout the course area.

START

FINISH LINE

Activity 1: Three-legged Run (Teams tie their two center legs together and run around 3 cones.)

Activity 6: Gunny Sack Race (Team members get into same sack and hop as quickly as they can to the finish line!)

Activity 2: Throw a Ball-a-Thon (Teams toss balls into the air 50 times while counting.)

Activity 5: Cycle Fun (Teams ride big wheel tricycles on circular or linear course.)

Activity 3: Sailboat Race (Teams blow small boats across a wading pool.)

Activity 4: Crazy Walk (Teams walk on a balance beam, or masking-taped line, backwards!)

Friendship Fudge

Ingredients:

2 cups (500mL) packed brown sugar

2/3 cup (160 mL) evaporated milk

1/2 teaspoon (2.5 mL) salt

1 1/2 cups (375 mL) chocolate chips

1 cup (250 mL) crunchy peanut butter

1 teaspoon (5 mL) vanilla extract

Butter for pan

Equipment:

8" (20 cm) square pan

medium-sized sauce pan

hot plate

measuring cups and spoons

table knife

Read and follow the directions. Share your fudge with a friend.

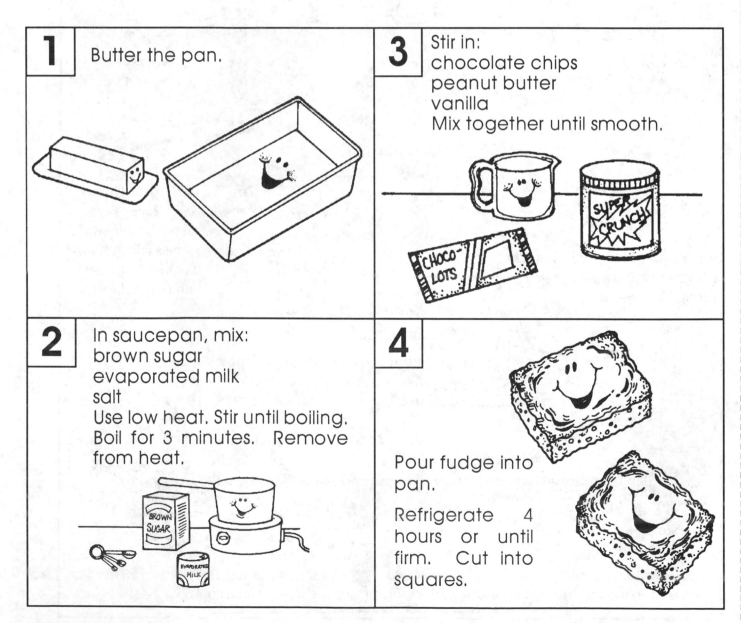

1 Butter the pan.

2 In saucepan, mix:
brown sugar
evaporated milk
salt
Use low heat. Stir until boiling.
Boil for 3 minutes. Remove from heat.

3 Stir in:
chocolate chips
peanut butter
vanilla
Mix together until smooth.

4 Pour fudge into pan.

Refrigerate 4 hours or until firm. Cut into squares.

Cooperative Cooking

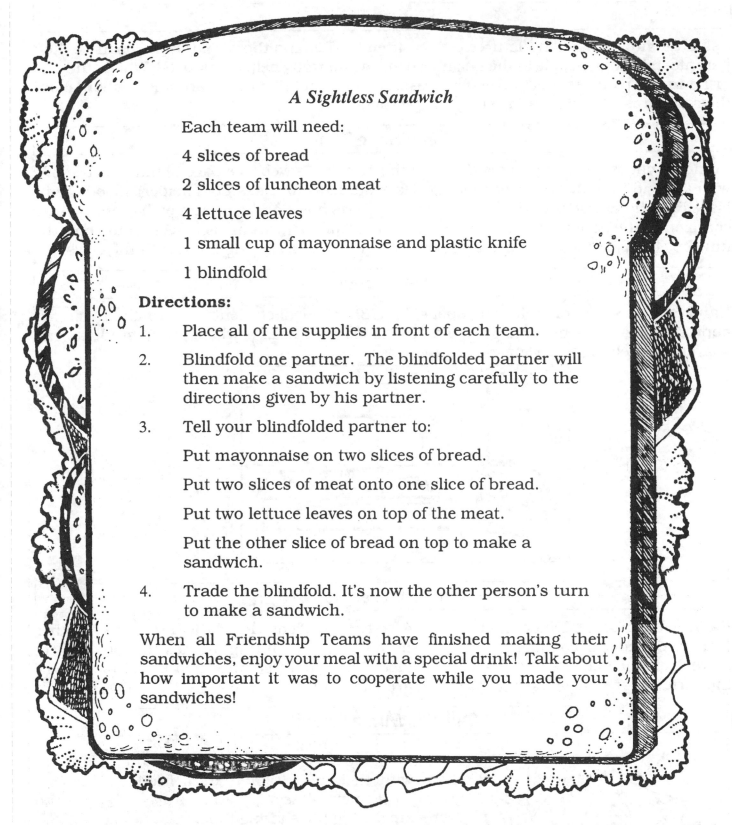

A Sightless Sandwich

Each team will need:

4 slices of bread

2 slices of luncheon meat

4 lettuce leaves

1 small cup of mayonnaise and plastic knife

1 blindfold

Directions:

1. Place all of the supplies in front of each team.

2. Blindfold one partner. The blindfolded partner will then make a sandwich by listening carefully to the directions given by his partner.

3. Tell your blindfolded partner to:

   Put mayonnaise on two slices of bread.

   Put two slices of meat onto one slice of bread.

   Put two lettuce leaves on top of the meat.

   Put the other slice of bread on top to make a sandwich.

4. Trade the blindfold. It's now the other person's turn to make a sandwich.

When all Friendship Teams have finished making their sandwiches, enjoy your meal with a special drink! Talk about how important it was to cooperate while you made your sandwiches!

Just For Fun! Make a large poster of the sandwich with the directions (#3) on it. While the students are cooperating to make their sandwiches, take pictures. Have the film developed and display around the sandwich poster in your classroom or hallway!

Homework Activities

Picture This!

Ask students to bring in pictures of their friends. Remind them that friends can be their parents, relatives, people in the neighborhood, community helpers, or pets! When students bring in the pictures, begin the next lesson by allowing them to share information about their pictures and friends. Display the pictures.

Let's Have Fun!

Students choose three fun activities from the Fun Times web (see page 6) that can be done with a friend that afternoon or evening. Have students (or classroom helper) fill out "Let's Have Fun" homework chart (p. 72). Take the charts home and have fun with friends! After completing the activities, students draw appropriate pictures in each section to show the fun they had! Students return and post the charts after sharing them with the class.

Helper Coupons

Hand out a sheet of helper coupons (p. 73) to each student. Have them fill out appropriately. Cut out and give to a designated friend. In a whole group students can share their helping experiences with the class.

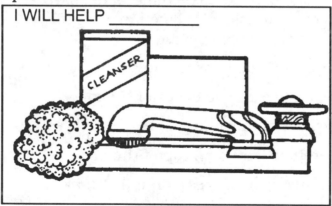

Same/Different Chart

Hand out the Same/Different chart (p. 74) to each student. Read the directions together and have students complete at home. Share the results during the next lesson. Collect all the returned charts and place in a folder. Place in a free time area for all to see how their friends are the same and how they are different!

Share It With a Friend!

Tell students to bring in a toy, game, or other activity to share with their new friends (from friendship teams) during the next lesson. Encourage students to cooperate during the sharing time.

Friendship Listening Center

Your students have learned a lot about what it means to be a friend. Here is an opportunity for them to show what they have learned in an exciting and unusual way! Follow the steps outlined to create a listening center for your class and other classes to enjoy!

Step One: Discuss the parts of a listening center: cassette tape recorder, cassette tape, listening headphones, and books with text to match words on the tape.

Step Two: Explain that as a class they are going to create a listening center. (Show them an actual listening center using books and tapes that have been checked out from the library.)

Step Three: Review what students have learned about friendship by brainstorming and writing their responses on chart paper.

> **We are all friends. Friends can be different. We have fun with our friends. We help friends. Friends can be different people or animals. Some friends are like me. Friends help us.**

Step Four: Using the chart as a guide, have students come up with the text for the listening center booklets. Write out the actual sentences on sentence strips. Read them with the class.

We are friends.

We like to help friends.

It is O.K. to be different.

Friends help each other.

Step Five: Have students sit close together and practice reading the sentence strips slowly and clearly. When they say them clearly and correctly, get ready to record their voices.

Step Six: For the recording, begin by having the class say, "Let's Be Friends... written, illustrated, and recorded by _____ class." To audibly signal listeners to turn the page, have one student ring a bell during the recording at the appropriate times.

(continued on next page)

Friendship Listening Center *(cont.)*

Step Seven: Play back the tape for all to hear. Have the class think of how they want to illustrate each page of their listening center read-a-long booklets. Brainstorm possible illustrations.

Step Eight: Copy the sentence strips onto 8 1/2" X 11" white paper, five times per sentence strip (so that you will create five separate "Let's Be Friends" booklets). Place the text near the bottom, long edge of paper.

Examples:

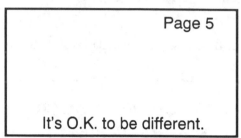

Page 5	Page 6
It's O.K. to be different.	A dog or cat can be a friend.

Step Nine: Distribute all the pages to be illustrated; students may use pencils, crayons, paints, or other mediums. Add a cover to each book (this can also be illustrated by students).

Step Ten: Collate the pages to create five "Let's Be Friends" booklets. Staple along left edge. Cover staples with tape.

Step Eleven: Set up a standard listening center with five headphone sets. Add a sign stating, "Come and listen with a friend!" Place a booklet by each headphone. Insert the class tape and let the fun begin!

Step Twelve: Share the fun with another class by inviting them to come to your Friendship Listening Center, or lend them your student-created tape and booklets to enjoy in their classroom!

A Friendship Fair

Now that your students have learned how to share, care, and cooperate with their friends at school and at home, celebrate by having a fun Friendship Fair. Follow the directions below to set up each Friendship Fair station. Students may go to the stations in one of two ways:

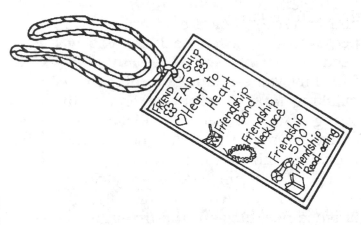

1. Rotate teams of students through each station for a set amount of time per station.

2. Make friendship badges (page 75) to be worn around student's necks which list the five stations. As they move around the room and choose a station to visit, that station's name is checked off by an adult.

Note: At each station area have at least one adult volunteer to act as monitor and to explain any necessary directions to complete the activities at the station.

The stations can be set up in the classroom, lunchroom, library, or even outside if it seems appropriate.

Station One: Heart To Heart

To review the concept that "friends have feelings," allow students to create friendship hearts. Students are given a large sheet of pink construction or butcher paper. An adult assistant helps them to fold paper and draw 1/2 a heart on the fold so that when the student cuts it out and opens it it will form a large heart. Students then use crayons to create a mosaic design on the heart. After coloring is done, students think of a statement to show that friends have feelings. The adult or students write their statements on the colored heart with a permanent black marker. Display the finished hearts around the school after the Friendship Fair!

Station Two: Friendship Band

To review the concept that "friends cooperate," create a friendship band by laying out a variety of musical instruments. Have an adult assistant help students select an instrument and practice playing it. As a group decide on a song they would like to sing accompanied by the musical instruments. Encourage students to cooperate with each other as they are playing and singing. After one song, trade instruments and try a different tune!

A Friendship Fair *(cont.)*

Station Three: Friendship Necklace

To review the concept that "friends have fun together," let the students giggle and laugh as they create a friendship necklace. For each necklace you will need a string 24" (60 cm) long; fruit-flavored o-shaped cereal; piece of masking tape (to tape the end of the string to form a "needle"). Place a bowl of dry cereal in the middle of the table. Provide each student with a taped string. Let them talk as they thread their necklace with cereal. Tie the finished necklace around the student's neck. They can then munch on their edible necklace while visiting the other friendship stations!

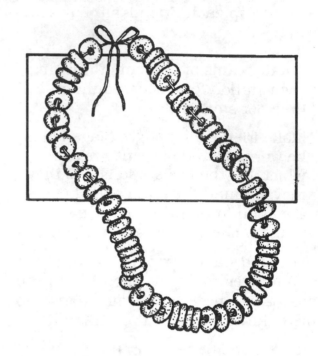

Station Four: Friendship 500

To review the concept that "friends care," students at this station will color and cut out race cars (page 76) to be used for a community project.

Prior to Friendship Day, select one of the causes from page 37 for your class or school to support. Create a race track from black butcher paper. Add yellow dashes down the center. Hang it in the hallway near your classroom or the front office area with the START and FINISH lines labelled. As a specified number of items is collected, add a race car with a child's name or a class's room number on it until the track is full.

Send a letter with the donations expressing your class or school's pledge to continue to care about their friends in the community.

Station Five: Friendship Read-a-thon

To review the concept that "friends share," create a cozy reading setting for students to pair up and read to each other. Have a variety of books from which the students can select!

Additional Activities

On these two pages you will find some additional ideas that may be used during the Friendship unit. You may need to adapt or change the activity to meet your classroom's needs.

Friendship Quilt

Divide a white cloth sheet into squares according to the number of students in the class. Cut along square lines, giving each student his/her own individual square. Using permanent marking pens, have the students draw their face and name on their square. Note: Be sure to warn them to draw their face and name away from the edges so that when the quilt is sewn together they won't lose any of their drawing! Ask a parent volunteer(s) to sew the squares together. Display the friendship quilt in the classroom or hallway!

Friendship Sack Lunches

Have students draw the names of classmates to form sack lunch teams. Provide a small brown bag for each teammate. Have them decorate their bags and write both their and their partner's names on the bag. Explain that each teammate will be making a lunch for their partner and bringing it to school to share with them on the following day. Send an information letter home with each student, as well as the bag they have decorated for their partner. Ask the parents to help their child make a sandwich and provide a fruit and dessert for the lunch sack. During lunch the next day, have the sack lunch teams switch their lunch sacks and eat together in the classroom, lunchroom, or outside. Ask a parent volunteer to make some punch as a lunchtime beverage. Happy eating!

Animal Friends

Animals are our friends, too. Ask students if they would like to bring in their animal friends from home. Make arrangements with the student's parents or other adult to bring in a pet friend for a show and tell time. Have the student tell the class about their special friend, including ways they take care, share, cooperate, and have fun with their friend! When the show and tell is finished, have the adult take the pet home.

Additional Activities *(cont.)*

Friendship Chain

Provide each student with a strip of colored construction paper that has been cut to an 8 1/2" X 2" (22 cm X 5 cm) size. Have each student write a sentence about a special friend on his/her strip. Allow students to share their sentences.

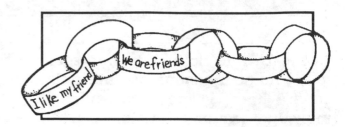

Curl and staple each strip onto a growing chain of friends! Hang the completed chain around a doorway, across the wall, or on a Christmas tree (if it's the right time of year!)

Friendship Books

Create blank folded books. Follow these directions:

1. First, fold a piece of 8 1/2" X 11" white paper in half once the long way.

2. Next, unfold and fold twice in the opposite direction.

3. Open the last fold; then cut a slit to the first fold only.

4. Open all the way. Then refold the long way and push out the center.

5. Continue pushing until the center comes together.

6. Crease and fold into a little book.

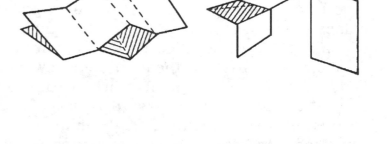

Students may use the eight blank pages to write a creative writing story about two imaginary friends. Have them illustrate their text and give their story a title. Have a friendship book sharing time and let students trade and read each other's books!

Friendship Calendar

Post a blank calendar in the classroom. Starting on the first day of the month, have a student write in the date and draw a picture or write a sentence about how he/she will be a friend to someone that day.

Larry 1	Shelly 2	Monica 3	Leonard 4			
I will help Joey read a book today.	I will help janitor clean lunch tables.	I will help Mr. Sterling give back papers.	I will cooperate with my soccer friends.			

"Friends Are Fun!" Bulletin Board

Objective

This bulletin board may be used to introduce or reinforce the concepts learned during this Friendship Unit. Adding student's work in each section will make the students feel good about themselves and the friends around them!

Materials

Background paper; construction paper; scissors; pushpins; stapler; yarn or string; pictures from pages 64-68; student's work to be displayed.

Construction

Reproduce and color pictures. Put up background paper and divide bulletin board into four sections using the yarn or string.

With pushpins or staples, attach a picture in each section and the heading, "Friends Are Fun," in the middle where the strings cross.

Suggested Uses

1. To use the bulletin board as an introduction activity, gather students around the board and discuss each picture and statement briefly. Explain that your class will be learning to be the best friends they can be.

2. Use the bulletin board to display student' work.

64

Friends can be different.

Cloud Pattern

*See suggested
activity, page 12.
Enlarge if desired.

Friendship Star Patterns

70

"I Care" Button Patterns

*See suggested activity, page 19.

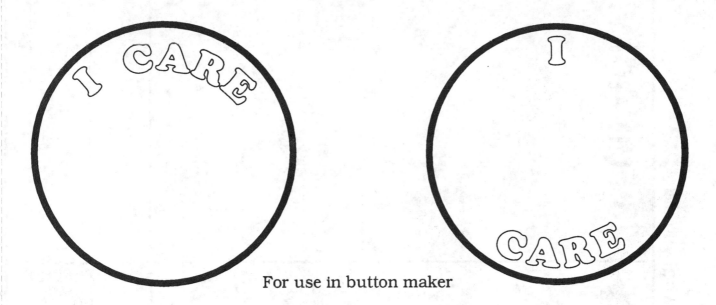

For use in button maker

For tagboard

Name _____

Let's Have Fun!

Draw pictures that show you having fun with your friends! Write what you did.

#1 Fun Activity	#2 Fun Activity	#3 Fun Activity

Helper Coupons

Fill in friends' names. Give them a coupon.

I will help_____

wash the dishes.

I will help_____

with homework.

I will help_____

play a game.

I will help_____

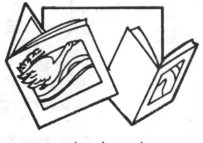

read a book.

I will help_____

clean up the bedroom.

I will help_____

by giving a hug and kiss.

I will help_____

take out the trash.

I will help_____

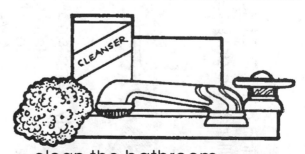

clean the bathroom.

Name

Same/Different

Find a friend at home or in your neighborhood to interview.
Fill in the blanks.

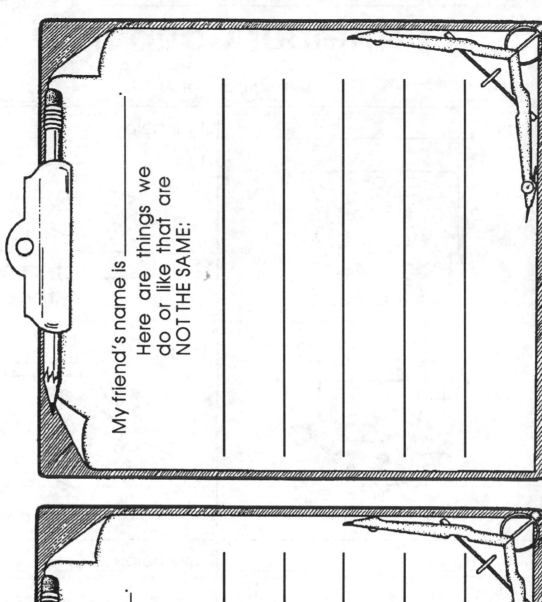

My friend's name is _____

Here are things we
do or like that are the
SAME:

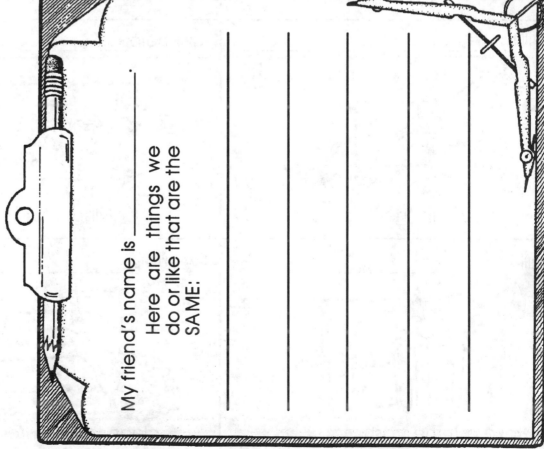

My friend's name is _____

Here are things we
do or like that are
NOT THE SAME:

Friendship Badges

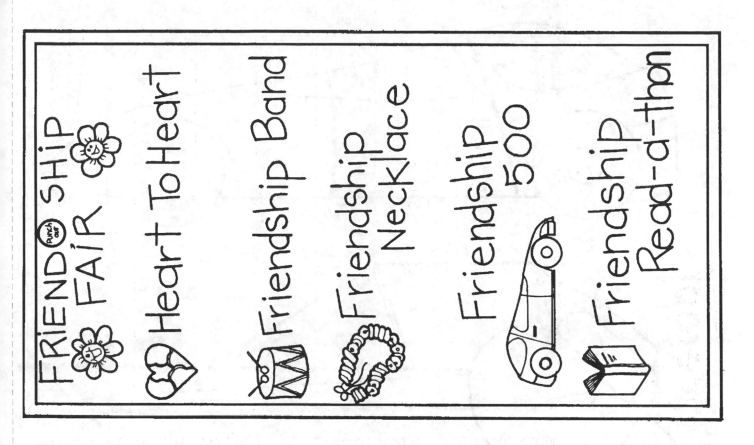

Friendship Race Cars

76

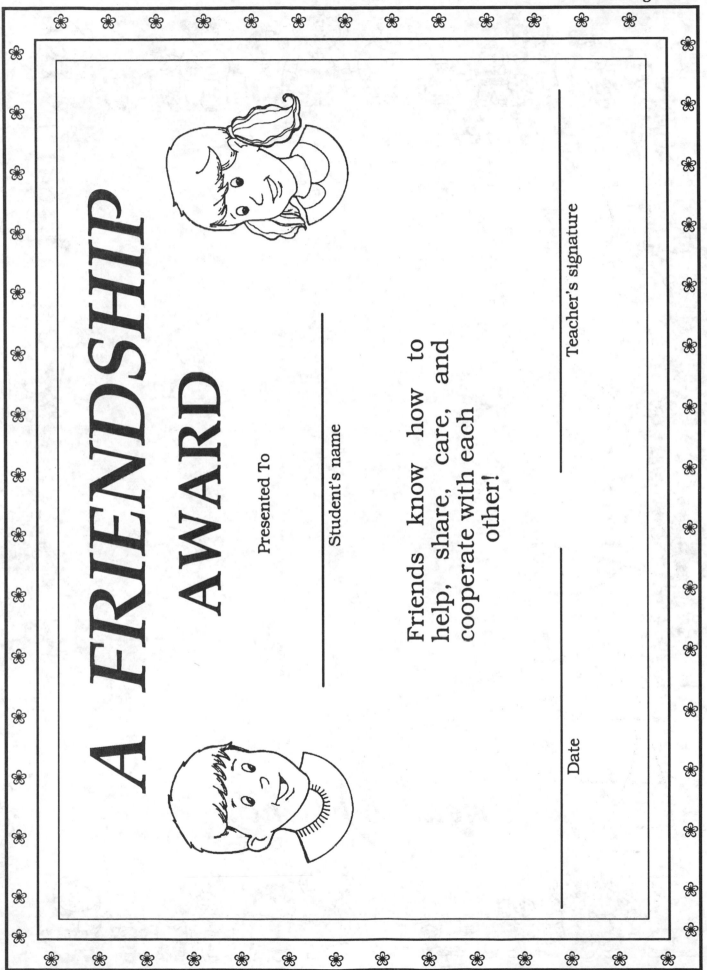

A FRIENDSHIP AWARD

Presented To

_____

Student's name

Friends know how to help, share, care, and cooperate with each other!

_____

Teacher's signature

_____

Date

A Note . . .

Friend to Friend!

78

Bibliography

Real Friends (People Stories)

Ahlberg, Janet and Allan. *The Jolly Postman.* Little, Brown, 1986

Cohen, Miriam. *Will I Have a Friend?* Macmillan, 1967

Gomi, Taro. *My Friends.* Chronicle Books, 1990

Viorst, Judith. *Rosie and Michael.* Macmillan, 1988

Waber, Bernard. *Ira Sleeps Over.* Houghton Mifflin, 1972

Zolotow, Charlotte. *The Hating Book.* Harper & Row, 1969

Make-Believe Friends (Animals or Other Characters)

Argent, Kerry. *Wombat and Bandifoot—Best Friends.* Little, Brown, 1988

Berenstain, Stan and Jan. *The Berenstain Bears and the Trouble With Friends.* Random House, 1986

de Brunhoff, Laurent. *Isabelle's New Friends (A Babar Book).* Random House, 1990

Freeman, Don. *Corduroy.* Viking, 1968

Lionni, Leo. *Alexander and the Wind-Up Mouse.* Random House, 1969

Lionni, Leo. *Little Blue and Little Yellow.* Aston Honor, 1959

Lobel, Arnold. *Best Friends—Frog and Toad Series.* Harper & Row.

Marshall, James. *George and Martha Series.* Houghton Mifflin.

Schenk de Regniers, Beatrice. *How Joe the Bear and Sam the Mouse Got Together.* Lothrop, 1990

Ziefert, Harriet. *Little Bunny's Noisy Friends.* Puffin, 1990

Suggested Titles for the Friendship Unit

Heine, Helme. *Friends.* Aladdin, 1982

Kellogg, Steven. *Best Friends.* Dial, 1986

Teacher Created Materials Related Resources

TCM107 *All About Cooperative Learning*

TCM108 *Great Games for Cooperative Learning*

TCM109 *Activities for Cooperative Learning*

TCM110 *Writing and Cooperative Learning*

TCM269 *Thematic Unit: Self-Esteem*

Answer Key

blue	red	blue	red
red	blue	red	blue
blue	red	blue	red
red	blue	red	blue
blue	red	blue	red

Page 45 - Friendly Fractions

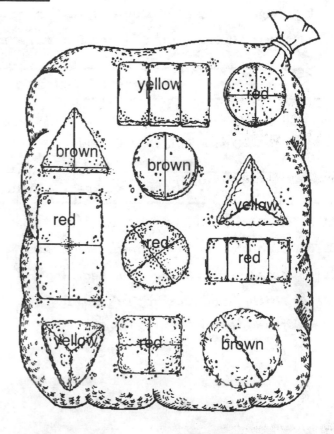